THIS JOURNAL BELONGS TO A VERY SPECIAL GIRL.
THAT GIRL IS YOU!

Make this come to life with your colors!

Autograph here!

Pragya Tomar
Cover Art by Giulia Iacopini
Inside art by Michela Fiori

Dedicated to Nishka
You were the answer
every time
I looked up at the skies
and asked for a
miracle...

Library of Congress Control Number: 2020937001

ISBN 978-1-7327528-9-4 (Paperback)

https://www.PenMagicBooks.com

PenMagic Books provides special discounts when
purchased in larger volumes for premiums and promotional
purposes, as well as for fundraising and educational use.
Custom editions can also be created for special purposes.
In addition, supplemental teaching material can be
provided upon request.

Hey Girl,

My name is Pragya, and I wrote this journal for you. I want to share my life experiences with you as I believe I can help you grow into a confident, inspiring and wise young woman. Having the right mindset and attitude can change your life. I wrote this journal with all my heart for my daughter, and she suggested I should share this with all the girls in the world. I want you to know I believe in you and want to help you explore and know yourself better so that you can lead a happy and fulfilling life.

Much love and appreciation,
Pragya Tomar

Hey Girl !

Remember

Hey Girl! This journal is a private place to share your own Unique Reality. It helps you explore, to be more aware about yourself, so write your ideas and opinions freely.

BY BEING YOURSELF, YOU PUT SOMETHING WONDERFUL IN THE WORLD THAT WAS NOT THERE BEFORE.

Fill this with your favorite colors!

— Elliot

My real name is:

The name I wish I had:

Friends call me:

My parents call me:

Languages I know:

My BFF:

My birthday is:

My age is:

I was born in: (country)   (State)

I wish I was from:

My biggest secret:

My signature:

Selfie!

Hey Girl! ABOUT YOU!

I am the ○ only ○ youngest ○ middle ○ oldest child

sketch yourself

My eye color is
- ○ green
- ○ blue
- ○ brown
- ○ black
- ○ other _____

My hair is
- ○ short
- ○ long
- ○ curly
- ○ straight

I am in grade_____

I love to wear

Time I wake up:

Time I go to bed:

Top five words that describe me:
- ○
- ○
- ○
- ○
- ○

I live with
- ○ both parents
- ○ one parent
- ○ grandparents
- ○ sibling
- ○ guardian

My Pet's name:

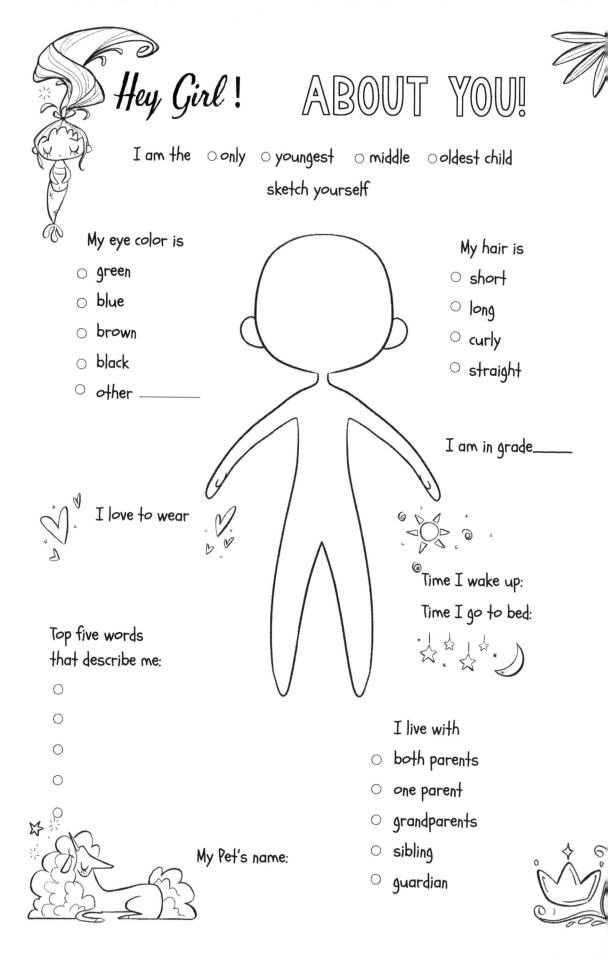

Hey Girl!

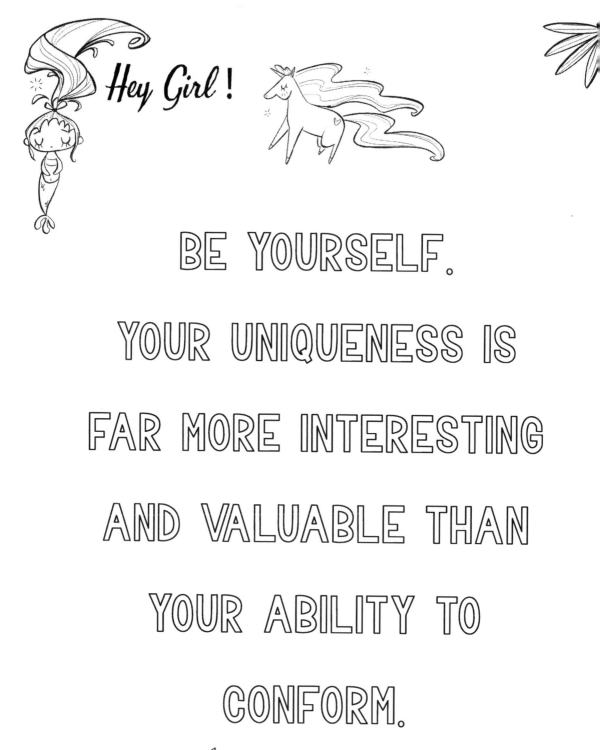

BE YOURSELF.
YOUR UNIQUENESS IS
FAR MORE INTERESTING
AND VALUABLE THAN
YOUR ABILITY TO
CONFORM.

*Color this
with love!*

TELL ME MORE

My favorite color is…

My favorite subject is…

I'm most happy when I…

My favorite movie is…

My favorite food is…

I really hate it when…

Yesterday, I…

Most people don't know that I…

If I won the lottery I'd…

Tomorrow, I will…

Right now, I feel very…

My favorite memory is…

Hey Girl!

I AM A MASTERPIECE!

Hey Girl! You are a masterpiece. There is no one in the whole world like you. You are so beautiful, so loving, so kind, and so wonderfully unique. There are dreams and ideas inside of you that no one else has ever thought of, and that the world so badly needs. Don't pretend to be anyone other than who you really are. You are powerful, beautiful, brilliant and brave. You're my definition of perfect.

Can you please color and say these affirmations out loud?

THE COOLEST

Season: _____

Movie: _____

TV show: _____

Book: _____

Store: _____

Ice Cream flavor: _____

School subject: _____

Game: _____

Month: _____

Food/snack: _____

Actor: _____

Actress: _____

Singer: _____

Fruit: _____

Pizza: _____

Outdoor Activity: _____

Restaurant: _____

NOT SO COOL

Season: _____

Movie: _____

TV show: _____

Book: _____

Store: _____

Ice Cream flavor: _____

School subject: _____

Game: _____

Month: _____

Food/snack: _____

Actor: _____

Actress: _____

Singer: _____

Fruit: _____

Pizza: _____

Outdoor Activity: _____

Restaurant: _____

I AM GRATEFUL.

Hey Girl! Gratitude helps you fall in love with the life you already have. Life is so short, and we spend so much time worrying about small stuff: stressing, comparing, wishing, and waiting for something new or greater instead of focusing on all the simple blessings that surround us everyday. Take a step back, and look at all those beautiful things you already have. Gratitude turns what we have into enough. It's through the practice of gratitude that we discover happiness, peace, and contentment in our hearts and our lives. Gratitude creates the most wonderful feeling.

It can resolve disputes.

It can strengthen friendships.

And it makes us better human beings.

Fill this out

each new day with new opportunities to be better.

I AM GRATEFUL FOR

Hey Girl !

Things to be grateful for:

A strength of mine for which I'm grateful:
_____

Something money can't buy that I'm grateful for:
_____

Something that comforts me that I'm grateful for:
_____

Something that's funny for which I'm grateful for:
_____

Something in nature that I'm grateful for:
_____

Something that changes I'm grateful for:
_____

A memory I'm grateful for:
_____

A challenge I'm grateful for:
_____

Something beautiful I'm grateful for:
_____

Things I love

Write and draw the things you love in the hearts below!

I love...

I love reading...

I love playing...

I love doing...

I love creating...

I love eating...

I love watching...

Hey Girl!

Tell the story of your family
Every family has a history.

photo or sketch of your family

My family consists of.:

_____

_____

_____

_____

My Family Story

Hey Girl!

I BELIEVE IN MYSELF.

"Because one believes in oneself, one doesn't try to convince others. Because one is content with oneself, one doesn't need other's approval. Because one accepts oneself, the whole world accepts him or her." - Lao Tzu

Hey Girl! The first secret of success is believing in yourself. You are stronger than you think, smarter than you know, and capable of more than you can imagine. One of our greatest weaknesses is our lack of faith in ourselves. Be patient and kind with yourself. Never let the opinions of others become the measure of your self-worth. Walk confidently in the direction of your dreams! Live the life you have imagined. Once you start believing in yourself, you are going to accomplish great things. Without struggle, there is no progress.

Write about a time when you did something you were afraid to try. How did you feel afterward?

How does it feel like when someone recognizes something you worked hard to do?

When you're feeling confident, what emotions do you experience?

Hey Girl!

I AM KIND TO MYSELF.

"The relationship with yourself sets the tone for every other relationship you have." – Jane Travis

Hey Girl! Treat yourself with kindness. Only you get to decide your worth. You, yourself, as much as anyone else in the entire world, deserve your love and kindness. Start loving yourself compassionately and completely. Be your own best friend. Encourage yourself, give yourself compliments, motivate yourself, and take good care of yourself. You're always with yourself, so spend time getting to know yourself, make a good relationship with yourself and enjoy the company.

It's time to:

I LOVE MYSELF
I RESPECT MYSELF
I ADMIRE MYSELF
I FORGIVE MYSELF
I ACCEPT MYSELF
I NURTURE MYSELF
TODAY IS THE DAY!

Hey Girl!

I AM THE AUTHOR OF MY STORY.

What if you had the power to write your own story? The story of how your life will be. Would you do it? Would you take charge of your story?

Hey Girl! You are the author of your own story. If you're stuck on the same page, remember at any moment you have the power to turn the page and start writing a new chapter. Your life is a book in progress, and you are the author. Get rid of the things that don't belong. Add more of the things that bring you happiness. Dream big and start writing your new adventure. Find the characters that are meant to help you on your journey. Embrace the middle chapters that are full of excitement and possibility. Write your own story because you are the only one who can. Write it with passion, with love! Try writing a good one.

No one else can tell your story, so tell it yourself.

No one else can write your story, so write it yourself.

Write your story!

Hey Girl!

Write your story!

Write your story!

Hey Girl!

I LET GO OF THINGS THAT NO LONGER SERVE ME.

"When I let go of what I am, I become what I might be." Lao Tzu

Hey Girl! Never spoil a good day by thinking about a bad day. You can spend your valuable time going over and over what could've happened or you could just choose to move on. Don't be afraid to walk away from things, places, and people that leave your soul heavy. Be mindful of where your thoughts are going. Stop replaying troubling memories. Stop worrying about the future.

Breathe. Be present. Then think of one happy thought you can think to feel better right here in this moment. Every new day we are born again. What we do today is what matters most. Starting today, you need to let go of what's gone, appreciate what still remains, and look forward to what's coming next. Life teaches us the art of letting go. When you have learned to let go, you will be joyful.

Give yourself time to: Accept what is,

Let go what was.

Have faith in what will be.

LET IT GO

Write some things that are
making you feel anxious or
upset in the balloons.
Close your eyes.
Imagine that you are holding the
balloons in your hand.
Imagine that you let them go.
Picture your worries floating
away with the balloons. Let it go.
Take a deep breathe and open your eyes.

Did your worries float
away with the balloons?

Hey Girl!

FRIENDS REFRESH MY SOUL

There are friends, there is family, and sometimes those friends become your family. Stick with friends who draw the magic out of you! There aren't many people that you just connect with. When you find those people, hold on tight to them.

Tell me more about your friends.

Name: _____

We are friends because

Photo or sketch

Name: _____

We are friends because

Photo or sketch

Name: _____

We are friends because

Name: _____

We are friends because

Name: _____

We are friends because

Hey Girl!

Draw a picture of someone you love.

IMAGINE you created your own sweet wishes for the people you love.

What would they say?

Hey Girl!

I AM STRONG, I DREAM BIG, I DO MY BEST!

Magic happens when you do not give up, even though you want to. The universe often falls in love with a stubborn heart. -J.M.Storm

Hey Girl, Please remember, nothing is permanent. You're not trapped. You have choices. Think of new ideas, make new plans, learn something new, imagine new thoughts, take new actions, meet new people, form new habits. All that matters is that you decide today and never look back.

Hey Girl! You got this! Success is not built on success. It's built on failure. It's built on frustration. It's built on not giving up. Try your best with no expectation and then let universe take care of it.

Let's keep trying!. Keep believing!.

Never give up.   Your day will come.

Every day is a new opportunity. Take a deep breath, smile and start again.

Write down goals you'd like to achieve in your life?
Be as specific as possible.

Hey Girl !

What is your dream job? What are five things you could do to turn your dream job into reality?

_____

_____

_____

_____

_____

_____

_____

Will you need to go to college for this career?

_____

_____

_____

_____

_____

_____

Do you know someone who has your dream job?

_____
_____
_____
_____
_____
_____

Can you research and find out what they did to achieve that?

_____
_____
_____
_____
_____
_____

Hey Girl!

I CHOOSE TO BE BRAVE LIKE A LION, EVEN IF ONLY FOR TODAY!

Be bold enough to use your voice, brave enough to listen to your heart, and strong enough to live the life you've always imagined.

Hey Girl! The greatest fear in the world is the opinions of others. A lion doesn't concern itself with the opinion of a sheep. The moment you are unafraid of the opinions of others, you are no longer a sheep. A great roar rises in your heart, the roar of freedom! Don't be scared to speak out. Hey girl, promise me you will not shrink yourself in order to make others feel comfortable. Don't base your self-esteem on other's opinions. Your actions will inspire others to dream more, learn more, do more, and become more. You are a leader!

Color this!

Hey Girl !

IMAGINE
You could wave
a magic wand.

What would you wish for?

_____

_____

_____

_____

_____

_____

_____

_____

IMAGINE
You could be
your favorite
superhero.

What would you do?

_____

_____

_____

_____

_____

_____

_____

_____

_____

_____

_____

Hey Girl!

I LOVE MYSELF!

"How you love yourself is how you teach others to love you." – Rupi Kaur

Hey Girl! When you love yourself, your soul lights up! You are automatically attracted to people who love, respect, and appreciate your energy. Everything begins with how you feel about yourself. You should eat like you love yourself. Move like you love yourself. Speak like you love yourself. Act like you love yourself.

Loving yourself starts with respecting yourself, which starts with thinking of yourself in encouraging ways. You, as much as anybody else, deserve your love and kindness. Inspire yourself, have faith in yourself, and love yourself. Never doubt who you are. Spend time exploring who you are. In the end, the only person you're ever going to truly live with is yourself.

To begin loving yourself start saying these affirmations out loud.

- I shall lovingly accept myself as I am right now.

- I shall appreciate all the beauty that makes me who I am.

- I shall regularly give thanks for everything I have.

- I shall trust in my ability to take care of myself, but I

  shall not be afraid to ask for help when I need it.

- I shall not criticize myself.

- I shall not criticize others.

- I shall forgive myself when I make a mistake.

- I shall be kind to others, without sacrificing my own needs.

- I shall take responsibility for my life.

- I shall love myself to the best of my ability.

Hey Girl!

I AM AWARE OF MY EMOTIONS.

Hey Girl! Emotional self-awareness is the ability to identify and understand your emotions and how they affect your behavior. Sensations and feelings are like waves in the ocean. Some come crashing in, while others roll in gently, but they always come and go. We can't stop the waves from coming, but we can be aware of their presence so, they don't knock us over. Inner peace begins the moment you choose not to allow anything outside of you to disrupt your emotions.

Try accepting your feelings without judgment.

Please remind yourself, you are not your emotions. Say this to yourself, silently or (when possible) aloud: "I can handle this emotion. I am strong and able to handle this wisely, easily, calmly."

All my FEELINGS

Share examples of when you've experienced these feelings!

A time I felt HAPPY was when _____

_____

A time I felt CALM was when _____

_____

A time I felt CONFUSED was when _____

_____

A time I felt NERVOUS was when _____

_____

A time I felt EMBARRASSED was when _____

_____

A time I felt ANGRY was when _____

_____

A time I felt SAD was when _____

_____

Hey Girl!

MY FEELINGS

Color the feelings on this page according to the chart.

COLOR	I FEEL THIS WAY...
green	Often
blue	Sometimes
yellow	Never/Hardly Ever

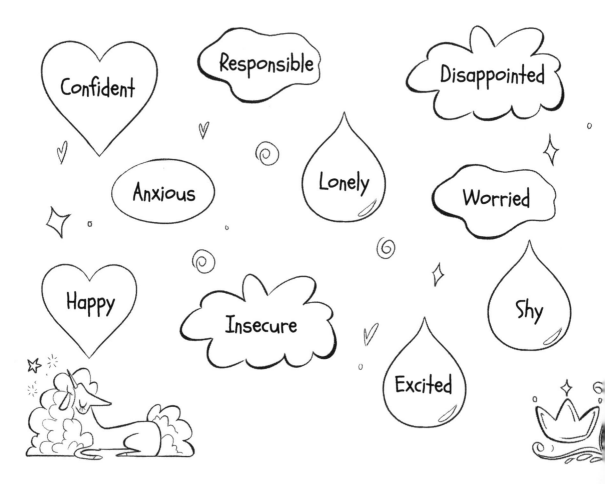

Hey Girl!

I FORGIVE. FORGIVENESS IS AN ACT OF SELF-LOVE

Hey Girl! It took me great deal of time to realize what it meant to forgive someone. I always contemplated how could I forgive someone who hurt me. But after a lot of soul searching, I realized that forgiveness is not about accepting or excusing someone's behavior. It's about letting it go and preventing it from disrupting your inner peace. Sometimes people hurt each other. It happens to all of us. Purposely or accidentally, regretfully or not. It's a part of what we are as people. The beauty is that we have the ability to let go, heal and forgive.

Forgive others, not because they deserve
forgiveness, but because you deserve inner peace.
— J.LH

IMAGINE
forgiving someone
who hurt you.

How would your life change?

_____

_____

_____

_____

_____

 _____

_____

LOVE

FRIENDS

CREATE

LAUGH

Have fun coloring this!

Hey Girl !

I FOLLOW MY HEART.

Hey Girl! If something excites you and scares you at the same time, it perhaps means you should do it. Have the courage to follow your heart and your instinct. Let your heart guide you when you're lost. Follow it wherever it may lead.

Listen to advice, but follow your heart and your dreams. Let no one tell you that they're silly or foolish. If something is important to you, pursue it. You deserve to be happy.

Try following your heart instead of your doubts and fears, and you will find the people and places that are truly meant for you.

Dreams for my future

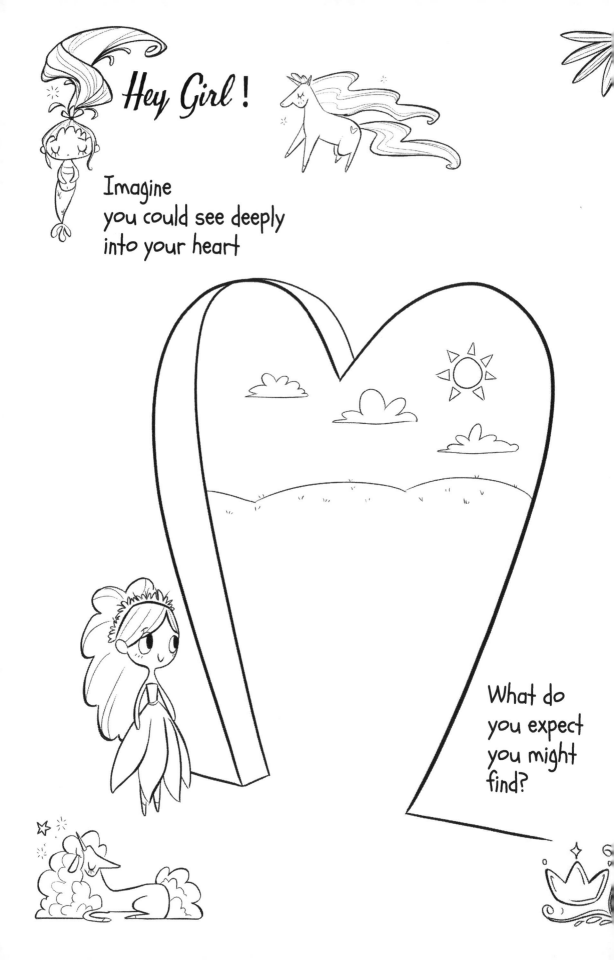

Hey Girl !

Imagine
you could see deeply
into your heart

What do
you expect
you might
find?

Imagine you could give the world some advice.

What advice would you give?

Hey Girl!

I AM READY TO TAKE THE FIRST STEP.

"A journey of a thousand miles begins with a single step."
Lao Tzu

Hey Girl! To achieve anything in life, start where you are. The first step of your journey might be intimidating, but it's also full of excitement and opportunities. It is full of great promises that could happen and faith that whatever is meant to happen, will happen.

The secret of having it all is believing you already do. Take that first step in faith. Don't over think. Don't worry. You don't have to see the whole flight of steps. Just take the first step.

The day you step outside of your comfort zone is the day your world will change. Have a dream and then take the first step!

Affirmation: I intend to push fear aside and take that first step.

Tell me, is there something that you always
wanted to do but were scared to try?

_____

_____

_____

_____

_____

_____

_____

_____

_____

_____

_____

_____

_____

_____

_____

_____

_____

_____

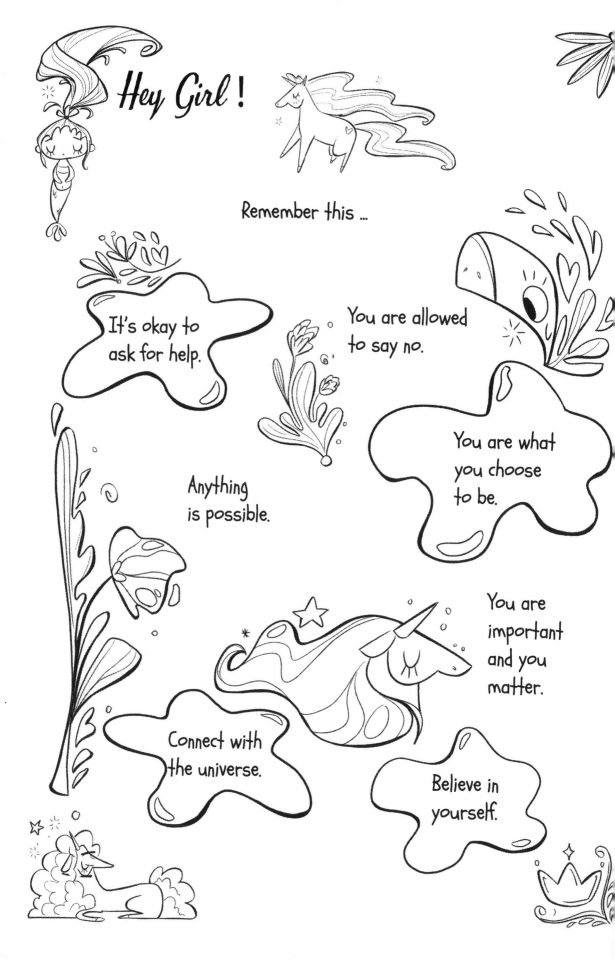

Hey Girl!

Remember this ...

It's okay to
ask for help.

You are allowed
to say no.

You are what
you choose
to be.

Anything
is possible.

You are
important
and you
matter.

Connect with
the universe.

Believe in
yourself.

Your mistakes don't define you.

You are worthy of great things.

You are so loved.

Feel Grateful.

You are enough.

You can overcome challenges.

Be inspired by the success of others.

Hey Girl!

I CELEBRATE LIFE AND SMILE.

Everyday of your life is a special occasion. Cherish every moment!

Hey Girl! You are meant to fill life with all the wonderful things that fill your heart with joy. You are meant to live in a way that lights your soul from the inside out. Celebrate your big and little wins. Grow everyday! Nourish yourself! Compliment others whenever you can. Make art. Life is meant to be lived. Take a deep breath of fresh air. Go for a walk under the open blue sky. Explore the wild – hug trees, watch the animals, enjoy the sunrise. Enjoy the small things life has to offer. Learn to appreciate quiet moments. Celebrate your health, your strength, your smile, your life.

Fill these hearts out:

I would LOVE
to learn more about:

I would LOVE
to go to:

I would LOVE to try:

LOVE
yourself
enough
to question
and learn.

I would LOVE
to let go of:

I feel LOVE
when:

I would LOVE
to read books about:

I would LOVE
to create:

Imagine you had
a net to catch a
favorite moment
in your life

Which would it be?

Hey Girl!

I AM CREATIVE.

Creativity is intelligence having fun! – Albert Einstein

Hey Girl! Being creative is being yourself. Creativity is the natural extension of our enthusiasm. Try to think up new things everyday! Create music, play with colors, write a poem, create a sculpture.! Being creative is seeing the same thing as everybody else but thinking of something different. The essence of life is in being creative! An essential aspect of creativity is not being afraid to fail. Creating makes one happy and excited about an adventure of making something unique. Try creating!
Try creating something today!

Write about what you enjoy creating!

I love creating...

Hey Girl !

I AM ENOUGH.

Hey Girl! Just in case you have forgotten: You matter. You are loved. You are enough! You were born being enough. Nothing you say or do will ever change that. You have what it takes. You are enough, just as you are. You are strong enough, brave enough and capable enough. You are worthy. It's time to stop doubting yourself and start believing in yourself. No one else sees the world like you and no one else holds the same magic inside. You are unique! It's time to start believing in the power of your dreams. You are ready. You are enough!

Tell me more

What is the best compliment you've ever received?

What do you see when you look in the mirror?

How do you think other people see you?

Hey Girl!

I AM PAINTING MY MASTERPIECE.

Hey Girl! Your life is your masterpiece; your own creation. You're the artist of your masterpiece. No one else gets to live your life. Paint your masterpiece, paint it with love, paint it with passion. You are the one who decides how to paint every little detail of your canvas— the colors, the texture, the strokes, and everything.

Don't be scared to try new things or add new colors because that's what your canvas is for. Use bold colors, make mistakes, start over whenever you want. This is your life and your masterpiece; create one with love, create one with kindness.

Draw a picture of yourself in your favorite costume

Hey Girl !

IMAGINE
That you could speak to your favorite character from a book.

Who would that be? What would you say?

_____

_____

_____

_____

_____

_____

_____

List the places you wish to go!

Hey Girl!

I CHOOSE POSITIVE THOUGHTS.

Positive thoughts create hopeful feelings and attract positive life experiences. A positive mind looks for ways a task can be done; a negative mind looks for ways it can't be done. Being positive doesn't mean that everything is good – it's changing your mindset to see the good in everything.

Hey Girl, put your positive pants on; train your mind to see the good in everything. Positivity is a choice. The happiness of your life depends on the quality of your positive thoughts. When you focus on the good, the good increases. A great day that starts with a positive thought invites encouraging events throughout the day. Cultivating positive thinking is not about expecting the best to happen, rather it is about accepting that whatever happens is for the best.

Hey Girl !

Positive Self-Talk

I felt good when...

I am proud of myself because...

I had fun when...

This makes me unique...

I like this about myself...

This was interesting today...

I learned from this mistake...

I love my....

I accomplished...

The best part of today was...

I feel strong when...

I am good at...

Hey Girl!

THE POWER OF YET

"I don't get it .... YET"

"I'm not good at this .... YET"

"I don't understand this......YET"

"This doesn't make sense .....YET"

"This doesn't work ....YET"

Hey Girl! Everything you don't know
is something you can learn!

It may not be easy, but it doesnt mean you're
never going to meet the challenge.

Tell me about the things that you can't do YET...

I can't do
this yet...

What can I do
to learn how?

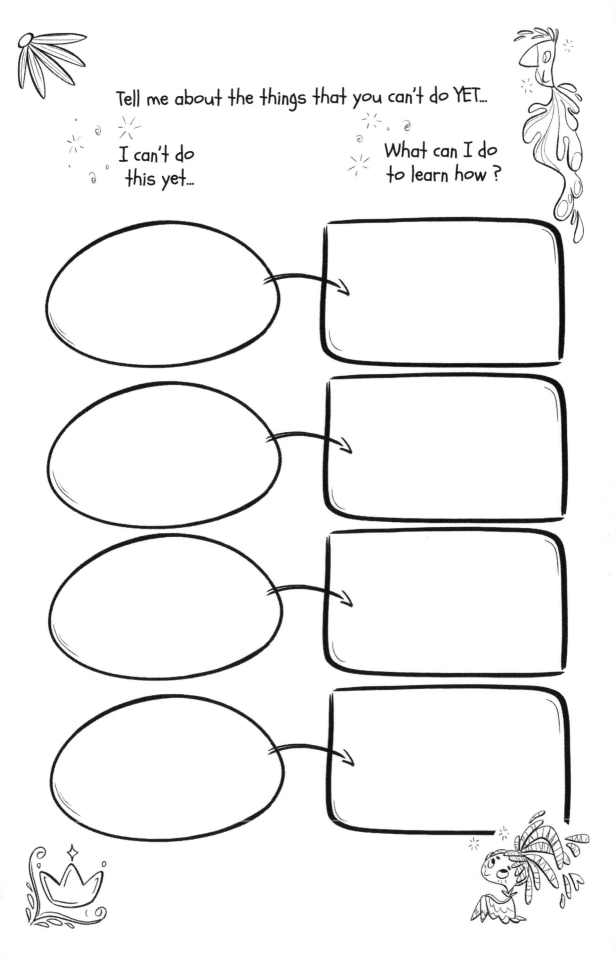

Hey Girl!

I AM WILD! I AM FREE!
I AM MYSELF!

"To shine your brightest light is to be who you truly are."

– Roy T. Bennett

Hey Girl! You are unique. You have different talents and abilities. You don't have to always follow in the footsteps of others. NO... You are here to create your own vision and then bring that vision to life. You are here to break away from normal, set new standards, shake things up. You are here to be yourself and to be different. You are here to live out your wildest dreams and create your own reality. You are here to follow your unique passions because what you can do, nobody else can. To be original, just try being yourself, as God has never made two people exactly alike.

FEEL

HELP

SEE

TRY

ENJOY

color this!

Hey Girl!

MY WORDS HAVE POWER!
I USE THEM WISELY.

"When words are both true and kind they can change the world."
– Buddha

Hey Girl! Good words bring good feelings. Practicing silence is the best course of action when someone doesn't value your words. If speaking kindly to plants helps them grow, imagine what speaking kindly to humans can do.

Words can hurt or they can heal. They can break a heart, or heal it. They can hurt a soul, or free it. They can crush dreams, or enliven them. They can create boundaries, or melt them.

Words are powerful. Choose them wisely.

Tell me about a time when you used harsh words?

1. How did it make you feel?

2. How did you make it right?

Hey Girl!

KINDNESS BEGINS WITH ME.

Ah. Kindness. What a simple way to tell another struggling soul that there is love to be found in this world. – A. A. Malee

Hey Girl! Be the one who makes others feel included. You never know what someone is going through. Be kind always. People may forget what you said. People may forget what you did. But then again people may never forget how you made them feel. A kind hug, a smile or few nice words can help a person more than you think. Your kindness can turn someone's life around. Be kind to your family, friends, and even strangers. You never know how much someone needed that long hug or listening ear. Be known for your compassion. Every deed of kindness grows the spirit and lights up the soul. Too often we undervalue the power of a hug, a smile, a kind word, a listening ear, or the smallest act of kindness. All of these have the promise to turn a life around.

Carry out a random act of kindness, with no expectation of reward. Color them as you do them.

Leave someone a kind note

Give a compliment

Give a hug

Pick up litter

Write a thank you letter

Write a positive note to a classmate

Volunteer

Hold the door open for someone

Donate old books and toys

Do a chore for your sibling or Mom

Help someone having a tough day

Forgive someone's mistake

Hey Girl!

I AM MINDFUL.

Hey Girl! Mindfulness is being aware, living in the moment, focusing on breathing, and paying attention to your thoughts as they emerge. Our life is shaped by our mind, for we become what we choose to think. Your mind will believe everything you tell it. Feed your mind with good thoughts. Feed it the truth. Feed it with care. Some days stink. Not everything is going to be how you want it. You'll get upset. But you can manage this feeling. You can slow down, take a few deep breaths, and pay attention to your feelings.

Hey girl, you need to know that whatever you are feeling is okay. Listen to your body. Notice the sensations you are having. Pay attention to your mind talking. Are the words supportive and understanding or rude? Are you being gentle to yourself? Let your breath be infused with gratefulness. Be thankful that you can breathe, eat, walk, focus, ask questions, and meditate. This is how we practice mindfulness. This is how we become aware of our minds.

In each oval, add something that makes you anxious that you need to let go.

I LIVE IN THE PRESENT.

Hey Girl! If our minds hold thoughts about the past or future, we are not truly loving the present. Stay here, be present in this moment. Replaying broken memories causes anger and distress. Worrying about future will create anxiety. Practice staying in the present. It will heal you. Living in present is the best practice to live your life peacefully.

Enjoy where you are at now. You are supposed to be right where you are. We are guilty of dwelling on negative thoughts about our lives. We get trapped into "where should we be" and all that does is cause stress and anxiety. Stay here. Stay present. Love this moment. Love yourself as you are.

Let's try staying engaged in the now.
Breath by breath,
let go of the expectation,
fear, regret and frustration.
Let go of the need for
constant approval.
You don't need any of it. – Surya Das

Affirmations to live in the present

Today will be a good day.

Everything will be okay.

I am in control of my life and feelings.

I have people that love me.

I have a lot to be grateful for.

Everything I need is within me.

Tomorrow will be better.

Hey Girl !

I AM PRESENT

Color them as you experience them

Smell a flower

Chase a butterfly

Have a picnic in the backyard

Look at the stars

Hug (for no reason)

Breathe deeply

Have a family group hug

Read a favorite book

Draw a rainbow

Hold hands and jump

Listen to the birds

Enjoy a warm bath

Pick wild flowers

Smile

Hey Girl!

I CHOOSE MY THOUGHTS.

Hey Girl! Your happiness depends on the quality of your thoughts. Choose your thoughts wisely, for they are the energy that shapes your life. Just imagine your mind is like a garden and your thoughts are the seeds. You get to choose what seeds you plant in it. You can choose to plant love, hope, and abundance, or you can plant the seeds of anxiety, fear, and jealousy.

We become what we give our time and attention to. When you fill your mind with thoughts of kindness, love, faith, hope, and joy, your reality will become all of these things. You will start to see love, hope and kindness in the world. You will begin to feel positive as you go about your day. You will notice more of the little joys of life. You've tried listening to your fears and doubts and they have never brought you happiness. It's time to start choosing love. It's time to start believing in yourself. Learn how to choose your thoughts the way you choose your clothes every day.

Instead of:
I'm a mess!
I'm a failure.
Why is this happening?

Try:
I am human.
I'm learning.
What is it teaching me?

What thoughts are on your mind?

Hey Girl!

MY MISTAKES TEACH ME.

"Anyone who has never made mistakes has never tried anything new."
Albert Einstein

Hey Girl! You are allowed to make mistakes. You are allowed to fail. Problems are guidelines, to show you the way! You are allowed to start over from scratch. You are allowed to change your mind. You are allowed to try over and over again. You are allowed to struggle. No path is ever a perfectly straight line. Your path will twist and turn in directions you never expected. Life will bring you unexpected highs and lows that make you stronger. You don't need to have it all figured it out right now because you will get where you are meant to be in time. To give up, is the easiest thing in the world to do. But, to persist when everyone would expect you to fall apart; that is true strength. Learn from every mistake, because every experience is there to teach you and shape who you are.

It's okay to make mistakes

Think of a time in your life when you made a mistake.
What happened?

_____
_____
_____
_____
_____

What did you do about it?

_____
_____
_____
_____
_____

What did you learn from your mistake?

_____
_____
_____
_____

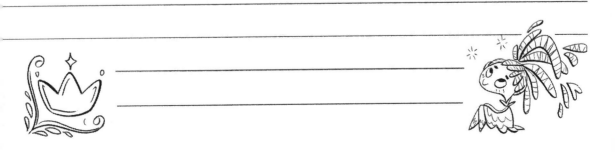

Hey Girl !

GRASS IS GREENER ON MY SIDE TOO!

"When you are content to be simply yourself and don't compare or compete, you will find respect." – Lao Tzu

Hey Girl! Every minute you spend wishing you had someone else's life is a minute spent wasting yours. There will always be someone who has a little more than you, and there will always be someone who has less. Stop comparing. Start accepting where you are right now. Because you won't ever be happy if you don't learn to love your imperfect, everyday life. The only person you should try to beat is the person you were yesterday.

Hey Girl! Don't compare your journey with others. We are all walking our own unique path. Comparison kills creativity. There is room for you. Nobody has your voice, your experience, or your mind. Happiness is found when you stop comparing yourself to others.

Hey Girl!

I AM AUTHENTIC.

Hey Girl! Authenticity is when you say and do things you actually believe. It is to know who you are and being brave enough to accept it and live it.

When you stop pretending to be anything other than who you truly are, and instead, put all of that energy into being yourself, your life will transform. You won't have to worry about fitting in, because you will be focused on simply being YOU! When you stop pretending to be anyone else, you will become your truest self and who you were meant to be. Authenticity is a practice – a conscious choice of how we choose to live. It's about being honest with your choice, the choice to let our true selves be seen.

Hey Girl! Try being authentic... be completely yourself that everyone else feels safe to be themselves too.

Self exploratory questions

What are you passionate about?

What makes you happy to be alive?

How are you making the world a better place?

I wish I knew more about...

When I grow up, I want to...

Something I want to invent to make life better is...

Hey Girl !

IMAGINE
That your deepest
hope will come true
this new year.

What would you wish for?

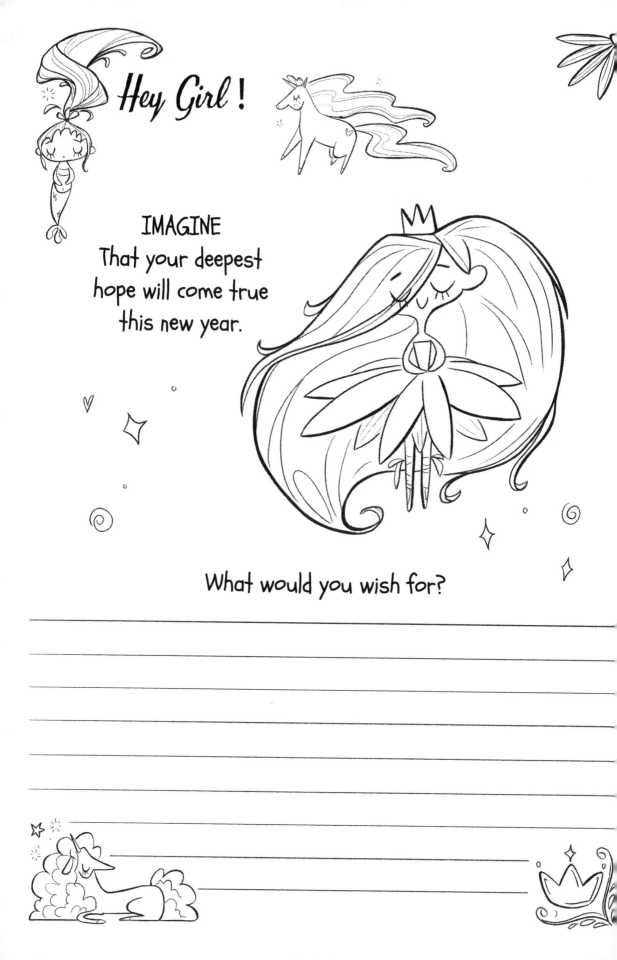

IMAGINE
You could express
something in your
heart that you longed
to say but were
afraid to.

What would
that be?

Hey Girl!

I ENJOY MY JOURNEY!

Hey Girl! Don't wait for everything to be perfect. Accept and embrace where you are in your journey. Even if it's not where you want to be. There is a purpose of everything that happens in our lives. You don't have to know what comes next. You don't have to have everything figured out right this moment. You don't need to know your entire story.

You are a living, changing, growing soul, riding through your unique and beautiful journey of life. And that's exactly what it is— a journey— and it wouldn't be a journey if you knew everything that was coming next. It wouldn't be a journey if you knew how it would all turn out in the end. So be patient with yourself and smile at the unknown, because your story is just starting to be written.

My best memories!

Hey Girl !

I AM PERSISTENT.

A river cuts through a rock not because of its power,
but because of its persistence.

Many of life's failures are people who did not realize how close
they were to success when they gave up. – Thomas Edison

Hey Girl! Be that girl who believes anything is possible and is willing
to work for it. You never know when you are minutes away from a
breakthrough.. That is why you keep going; that is why you keep trying.
That is why when you fall down, you get back up. Because the truth is
too many people quit before even giving themselves a real chance.
They stop because things aren't happening fast enough or aren't
working out how they planned.
Hey Girl, remember, some of the most important things in the world
have been accomplished by people who kept on trying when there
seemed to be no hope at all. All good things take time.
Be patient, and your time will come too.

Fill this out

WHAT INSPIRES ME?

Music inspires me!

Hey Girl!

Imagine
you could ask a bird
to deliver a special message...

What would it
be and to
whom would
you send it?

Imagine you planted your dreams

What would you hope to grow?

Hey Girl!

READING IS FUN!

A girl who reads will be
an adult who thinks!
Reading is to the mind
what exercise is to the body.

The more you read, the more you will know.
Books add soul to the universe, wings to the mind,
flight to the imagination, and life to everything.
The more you learn, the more places you'll go.
I do believe something magical happens when
you read a good book.
– Dr. Seuss

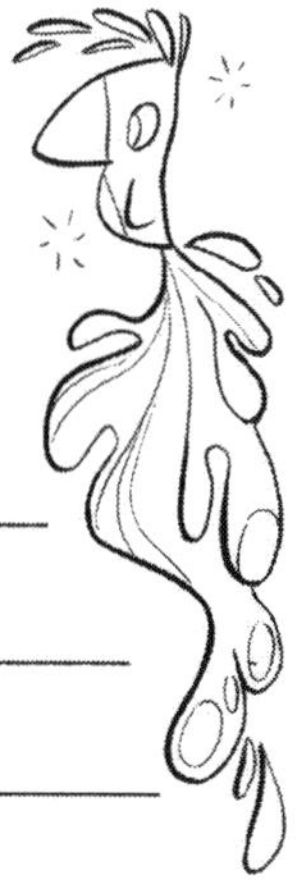

Name your favorite book. Why do you like it so much?

_____

_____

_____

_____

_____

_____

_____

_____

_____

_____

_____

_____

_____

_____

_____

_____

_____

_____

_____

_____

Hey Girl!

Let's talk about 11 habits of successful girls!

1. They live in a state of gratitude.

2. They have the power to control their mind and thoughts.

3. They educate themselves.

4. They make mistakes, learn from them and move on.

5. They know the importance of self care and health.

6. They know the importance of being independent.

7. They smile and laugh a lot.

8. They make goals and stick to them with hard work

   and perseverance.

9. They support other girls and enjoy their success.

10. They help others with kindness.

11. They are authentic.

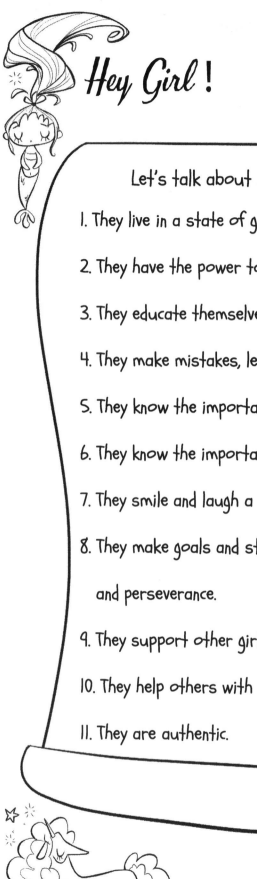

Hey Girl! Hope you enjoyed going through this journal and found some value in my suggestions.

If you would like to get in touch with me, please email me PenMagicBooks@gmail.com

Much love and appreciation,
Pragya Tomar

Made in the USA
Middletown, DE
11 December 2020